I SPY

EXTREME CHALLENGER!

A BOOK OF PICTURE RIDDLES

Photographs by Walter Wick

Riddles by Jean Marzollo

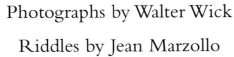

Cartwheel
B·O·O·K·S ®

SCHOLASTIC INC.

New York   Toronto   London   Auckland   Sydney
Mexico City   New Delhi   Hong Kong   Buenos Aires

To Adkins Isaac Word,
James Adkins Word

W.W.

For Drayton and Sam 1999
and Elizabeth and Michael 2000

J.M.

Book design by Carol Devine Carson

Go to www.scholastic.com for Web site information
on Scholastic authors and illustrators.

"Make Believe" and "Odd and Ends" from *I Spy* © 1992 by Walter Wick; "Christmas Crafts" from
I Spy Christmas © 1992 by Walter Wick; "Creepy, Crawly Cave" and "The Laughing Clown" from
I Spy Fun House © 1993 by Walter Wick; "Masquerade," "The Mysterious Monster," and
"The Toy Box Solution" from *I Spy Mystery* © 1993 by Walter Wick; "Monster Workshop" and "Yikes!" from
I Spy Fantasy © 1994 by Walter Wick; "Old-Fashioned School" from *I Spy School Days* © 1995 by Walter
Wick; "A Secret Cupboard" from *I Spy Spooky Night* © 1996 by Walter Wick.
All published by Scholastic Inc.

Library of Congress Cataloging-in-Publication available

0-439-19900-X (pob)

12 11 10 9 8 7 6 5 4 3 2   5 6 7 8 9/0
Printed in Malaysia   46

Reinforced Library Edition
ISBN: 0-439-68421-8
This edition, March 2005

TABLE OF CONTENTS

Picture riddles fill this book;
Turn the pages! Take a look!

Use your mind, use your eye;
Read the riddles — play I SPY!

I spy two clothespins, a busted clock tower,

Five jacks, a pie, Pegasus, a flower;

Two gears, two dice, two buns, a car,
A stern octagon, and the shadow of a star.

I spy a camera, a sewing machine,
A chain, a hammer, and 113;

Three lions, a ruler, a bottle of glue,
An elephant's trunk, and a buffalo, too.

I spy a saddle, a backwards B,
A Ferris wheel, and a tiger T;

A ladybug, a ticket, a goat,
Eight H's, three tees, and a photographer's coat.

I spy two pyramids, a baseball, a snail,

Three 22's, and a musical scale;

Four buttons, an arrow, and Harry's test,
A top, a whip, a compass, and BEST.

I spy a fishhook, a fingernail clipper,
A trophy, a timer, the top of a zipper;

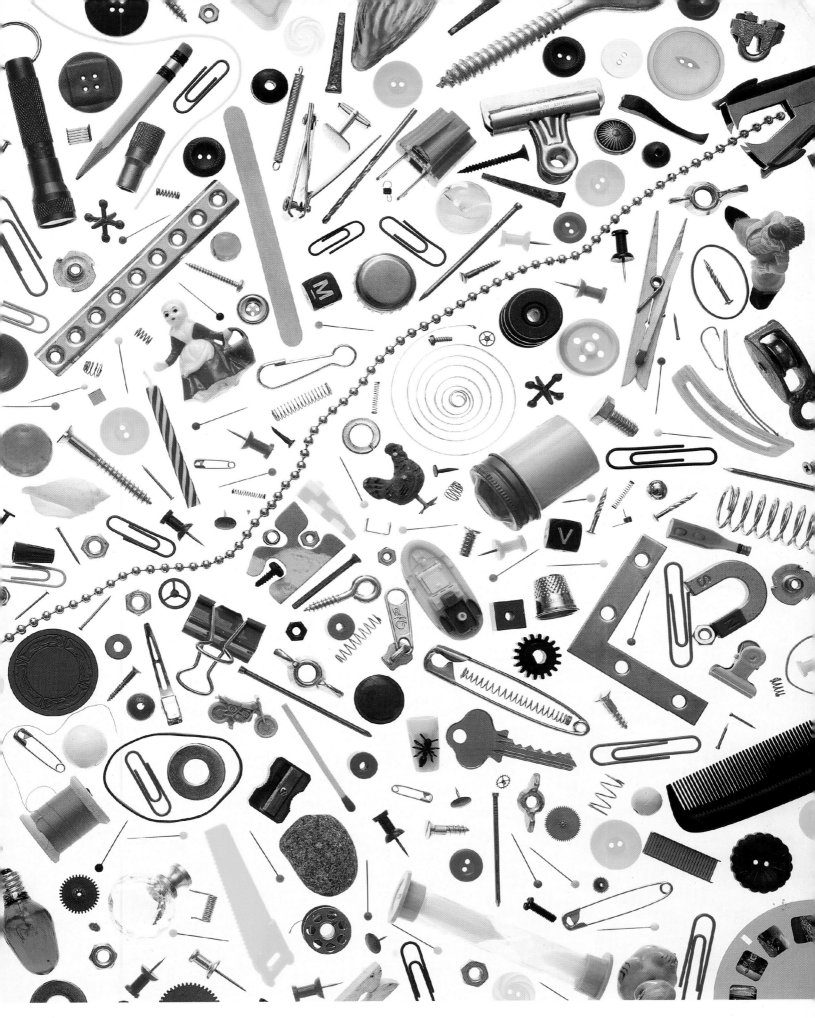

A bent straight pin, two bubbles, a bell,
Five erasers, a needle, a sword, and a shell.

I spy two thimbles, two timers, two dice,
Four birds, three tops, two jacks, six mice;

A pig, a nut, a guitar, an ace,
A wrench, and a missing bottle's space.

I spy a sharpener, a shoelace, a kitten,

Tape, a crayon, two gloves, and a mitten;

Three fancy dogs, a rocking-horse mane,
Two quilted stars, and a man in a plane.

I spy a gyroscope's shadow of blue,
A flamingo, two springs, and a kangaroo;

A hook, a toothbrush, a cat, a key,
A stegosaurus, and a sword from the sea.

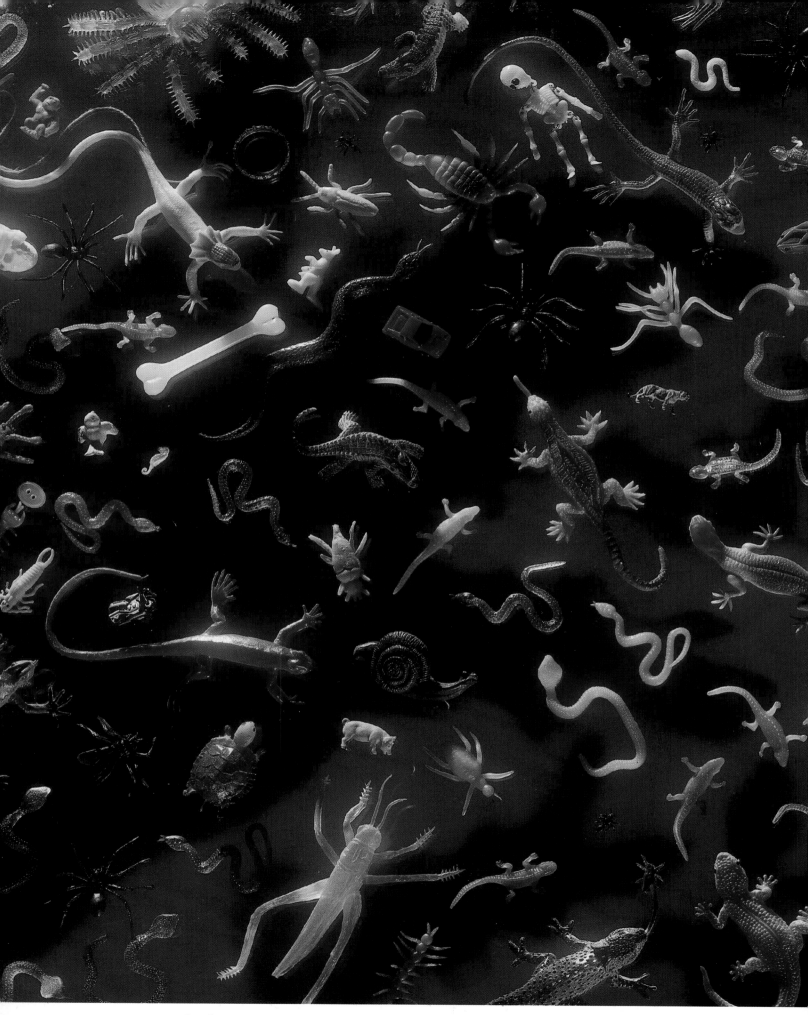

I spy a lobster, a pig, a guitar,

Two skulls, a button, a spring, a car;

Eleven spiders, a rabbit, a cat,
A woolly mammoth, and a shadowy bat.

I spy a clothespin, a button that's red,

A thimble, a nail file, a wee turtle's head;

Three pair of earrings, four bow ties,
A moustache, a frog, and two mousey eyes.

I spy a thumbtack, a pig, bear ears,
A spoon, a heart, a 3, and three gears;

Two button eyes, puffball shoes,
Two forked tongues, and sad blue ooze.

I spy a windmill, a compass, a cane,

An arrowhead, a lunchbox, a chain;

A xylophone, two keys, three bases,
Binoculars, and two starry places.

EXTRA CREDIT RIDDLES

Find the Pictures That Go With These Riddles:

I spy an airplane, a face with no hands,

A chicken, a cherry, and six rubber bands.

I spy two leaves, a black guitar,

XYLOPHONE, and a little blue star.

I spy a fan, a fish, six 4's,

A paper clip, and three dinosaurs.

I spy a football, a repeated phrase,

Two acorns, two pumpkins, and ten sunny rays.

I spy a flyswatter, a mouse, a dog,

An exclamation point, and a frog.

I spy a doll, three coins that shine,

Two question marks, and a division sign.

I spy a bag, a paper-dot tail,

Two plastic bows, a pin, and a nail.

I spy a giraffe and an ape for the zoo,

A marble, two mice, and a motorcycle, too.

I spy a yellow musical note,

Fourteen marbles, a brush, and a boat.

I spy a motorcycle, a lovely pearl ring,

A single eyeball, and a brown-and-gold wing.

I spy a needle, three windows of red,

Antlers, five fans, and a little elf's head.

I spy a clothespin, a spool of thread,

LA ARAÑA, a bear, and UNCLE NED.

Write Your Own Picture Riddles

There are many more hidden objects and many more possibilities for riddles in this book. Write some rhyming picture riddles yourself, and try them out with friends.

About the Creators of I Spy

Jean Marzollo has written many award-winning children's books, including eleven I Spy books and seven I Spy Little books. She has also written: *I Love You: A Rebus Poem; Ten Cats Have Hats; I Am Water; I Am a Star; In 1492; Happy Birthday, Martin Luther King; Pretend You're a Cat; Close Your Eyes; Soccer Sam; How Kids Grow; Thanksgiving Cats; Home Sweet Home; Sun Song; Mama Mama; Papa Papa;* and *Do You Know New?* With her grown sons she has co-authored *Football Friends, Hockey Hero, Basketball Buddies,* and *Baseball Brothers.* For nineteen years, Jean Marzollo and Carol Devine Carson produced Scholastic's kindergarten magazine, *Let's Find Out.* Ms. Marzollo holds a master's degree from the Harvard Graduate School of Education. She is the 2000 recipient of the Rip Van Winkle Award presented by the School Library Media Specialists of Southeastern New York. She lives with her husband, Claudio, in Cold Spring, New York.

Walter Wick is the photographer of the I Spy books. He is author and photographer of *A Drop of Water: A Book of Science and Wonder,* which won the Boston Globe/Horn Book Award for Nonfiction, was named a Notable Children's Book by the American Library Association, and was selected as an Orbis Pictus Honor Book. *Walter Wick's Optical Tricks,* a book of photographic illusions, was named a Best Illustrated Children's Book by *The New York Times Book Review,* was recognized as a Notable Children's Book by the American Library Association, and received many awards, including a Platinum Award from the Oppenheim Toy Portfolio, a Young Readers Award from *Scientific American,* a *Bulletin* Blue Ribbon, and a Parents' Choice Silver Honor. Mr. Wick has invented photographic games for *Games* magazine and photographed covers for books and magazines, including *Newsweek, Discover,* and *Psychology Today.* A graduate of Paier College of Art, Mr. Wick lives with his wife, Linda, in New York and Connecticut.

Carol Devine Carson, the book designer for the I Spy series, is the art director for a major publishing house in New York City.

The Story of *I Spy Extreme Challenger!*

The I Spy Challenger! books have been created in response to those children who have found every single thing in every I Spy book, including items listed in the Extra Credit riddles. These kids demanded harder riddles, so for *I Spy Super Challenger!*, Walter Wick and I selected the pictures with the most little things in them because they seemed to us the hardest to probe. Kids rose to the challenge, found everything, and asked for another Challenger! book. For *I Spy Gold Challenger!*, we matched our favorite I Spy photos with harder riddles, and once again, kids relished the book and asked for more. "What would you call it?" I asked kids when I visited schools. One day in 1998, a second grader at Primrose School in Somers, NY, suggested *I Spy Extreme Challenger!* Quickly, I whipped out a pen and wrote down the title, but, unfortunately, not the child's name. Whoever you are, wherever you are, thank you!

For this book, Walter Wick and I selected a variety of photos that are extreme in some wonderful way: fancily far-out, interestingly intense, amazingly imaginative, complicatedly complex, or, in some cases, just plain weird. As with all the I Spy books, we hope this book will inspire children to look at the world more carefully, use language more vividly, and think more creatively.

Acknowledgments

We would like to thank the following hard-working I Spy hunters for testing the riddles in this book: Kayla Allen, Melanie Bozsik, Chris Brennan, Jody Dew, Richard Donohue, Ian Gallagher, Brendan Galvin, Max Garfinkle, Kimberly Hyatt, Stefan Jimenez, Brian Levine, Michael Lyons, Amber McCoy-Snapp, Samuel Mell, Olivia Seymour, Kaitlyn Shortell, Darius Szkolnicki, Averyann Zuvic, and their third-grade teacher, Nancy Radtke; Michelle, Jennifer, and Donna Cotennec; Chris and Molly Nowak; Phoebe Zoe Little; Claudio Marzollo; and, once again, David Marzollo for his extremely creative output.

Jean Marzollo and Walter Wick

Other I Spy books:

I SPY: A BOOK OF PICTURE RIDDLES

I SPY CHRISTMAS: A BOOK OF PICTURE RIDDLES

I SPY FANTASY: A BOOK OF PICTURE RIDDLES

I SPY FUN HOUSE: A BOOK OF PICTURE RIDDLES

I SPY GOLD CHALLENGER!: A BOOK OF PICTURE RIDDLES

I SPY MYSTERY: A BOOK OF PICTURE RIDDLES

I SPY SCHOOL DAYS: A BOOK OF PICTURE RIDDLES

I SPY SPOOKY NIGHT: A BOOK OF PICTURE RIDDLES

I SPY SUPER CHALLENGER!: A BOOK OF PICTURE RIDDLES

I SPY TREASURE HUNT: A BOOK OF PICTURE RIDDLES

And for the youngest child:

I SPY LITTLE ANIMALS

I SPY LITTLE BOOK

I SPY LITTLE CHRISTMAS

I SPY LITTLE LETTERS

I SPY LITTLE NUMBERS

I SPY LITTLE WHEELS

Also available:

I SPY SCHOOL DAYS CD-ROM

I SPY SPOOKY MANSION CD-ROM

I SPY JUNIOR CD-ROM

I SPY JUNIOR: PUPPET PLAYHOUSE CD-ROM

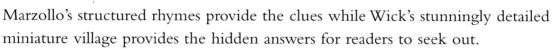

Reviews and Praise for I Spy

For *I Spy Treasure Hunt:*

Marzollo's structured rhymes provide the clues while Wick's stunningly detailed miniature village provides the hidden answers for readers to seek out.

School Library Journal

For *I Spy Gold Challenger!:*

The I Spy concept is a deceptively simple one — look for particular items in meticulously arranged photos that are often startling in their artistry.

The Hamilton Spectator

For *I Spy Super Challenger!:*

The trademark rhyming riddles lead sharp-eyed readers to objects in crisp photographs. Wick's painstakingly prepared illustrations — bright, elaborate, and wonderfully thematic — strike a great balance between shape and color.

Booklist

For the Educational Value of the I Spy Books:

Kids find I Spy engaging because it builds on their excellent visual discrimination skills. It also challenges them incrementally with some initial success virtually guaranteed. Good teachers provide for instruction this way — and it works! Another appeal of I Spy, besides the sheer beauty of Walter Wick's photographs, is their uniqueness. They capture our attention because they are different and interesting. Brain research tells us that learners respond to novelty. As children respond to I Spy, they improve their reading, writing, rhyming, critical thinking, and vocabulary skills.

Dr. Joanne Marien,
Assistant Superintendent
Curriculum and Instruction
Somers Public Schools
Somers, NY